NO OTHER ROME

AKRON SERIES IN POETRY

AKRON SERIES IN POETRY
Mary Biddinger, Editor

Heather Green, *No Other Rome*
Sean Shearer, *Red Lemons*
Annah Browning, *Witch Doctrine*
Emily Corwin, *Sensorium*
Kimberly Quiogue Andrews, *A Brief History of Fruit*
Joshua Harmon, *The Soft Path*
Oliver de la Paz, *The Boy in the Labyrinth*
Krystal Languell, *Quite Apart*
Brittany Cavallaro, *Unhistorical*
Tyler Mills, *Hawk Parable*
Caryl Pagel, *Twice Told*
Emily Rosko, *Weather Inventions*
Emilia Phillips, *Empty Clip*
Anne Barngrover, *Brazen Creature*
Matthew Guenette, *Vasectomania*
Sandra Simonds, *Further Problems with Pleasure*
Leslie Harrison, *The Book of Endings*
Emilia Phillips, *Groundspeed*
Philip Metres, *Pictures at an Exhibition: A Petersburg Album*
Jennifer Moore, *The Veronica Maneuver*
Brittany Cavallaro, *Girl-King*
Oliver de la Paz, *Post Subject: A Fable*
John Repp, *Fat Jersey Blues*
Emilia Phillips, *Signaletics*
Seth Abramson, *Thievery*
Steve Kistulentz, *Little Black Daydream*
Jason Bredle, *Carnival*
Emily Rosko, *Prop Rockery*
Alison Pelegrin, *Hurricane Party*

Titles published since 2012.
For a complete listing of titles published in the series,
go to www.uakron.edu/uapress/poetry.

NO OTHER ROME

Heather Green

The University of Akron Press
Akron, Ohio

ISBN: 978-1-62922-206-6 (paper)
ISBN: 978-1-62922-216-5 (ePDF)
ISBN: 978-1-62922-217-2 (ePub)

A catalog record for this title is available from the Library of Congress.

∞ The paper used in this publication meets the minimum requirements of ANSI/NISO
z39.48–1992 (Permanence of Paper).

Cover image: Kevin Francis Gray, *Greek Onyx Girl* (detail), 2018. © Kevin Francis Gray,
courtesy Pace Gallery. Photo: Kevin Francis Gray Studio 2020
Cover design by Amy Freels.

No Other Rome was designed and typeset in Garamond with Hypatia Sans titles by Amy Freels
and printed on sixty-pound natural and bound by Bookmasters of Ashland, Ohio.

Affordable
Learning Initiative
THE UNIVERSITY OF AKRON

Produced in conjunction with the University
of Akron Affordable Learning Initiative.
More information is available at
www.uakron.edu/affordablelearning/.

I am closer to you
Than land and I am in a stranger ocean
Than I wished.

—Barbara Guest, from "Parachutes, My Love,
  Could Carry Us Higher"

CONTENTS

IV

I

IF ANYTHING IS EVERLASTING IT CAN ONLY BE ONE THING

Early on, learned from Prince, parties weren't meant to.

But there is the subjunctive continuous, meant to last. We party. We keep going.

He was the last love on the last island, in the last channel-blasted reef.

The saddest words: *the last time.*

The last great auk.

Please last.

My Dad's last days. He was freezing and bearded in a hospice like a motel, the last rasping breaths.

He used to say: second is just the first person to finish last, or something like that.

From day to day / To the last syllable of recorded time

Some say grief is the last way you get to love someone, but in truth the dead become our close companions, even in joy.

Will anybody see the last flowering of the last nacred sea anemone?

I can't undo what I've already done. I'd go back in a flash.

Trees *sprinting up the hill* in search of cooler clime will last a little longer, but the hill is a cone with very little space up top, and only so high.

PROVINCIAL TIME

Resentment turned my cell nuclei into fake news.

The message spread like a rumor, became a dark star

Visible by ultrasound. I was prescribed a program

Of *wholeness, radiance, harmony,* the first achieved

Through surgery. My work became secondary.

In the white room of radiation, *Purple Rain*

On the sound system, hands over head, I held still.

I only want: cool tears made me human. On Fridays,

Throughout the initial smash and grab, I reclined

In a chair, drip line in my chest port, reading

About a young Tristan Tzara playing chess with Vinea

In the woods. At night I lay fetal with the dog

And tried to dream. One year gone, and I'm almost

Re-alive. Just before all this, Prince died. I cried,

And the next night, Graham arrived—her foxes,

Bots, Paris uprising 1968, utopian only in retrospect—

Embodied, to describe the artist's eye. Who can

See into the dark and, in singing, change the seen?

ARISTOTLE IS A SKELETON

The skeleton called out for sets of bones
to fill the hole, but then you reached your arm in,
your fingers stretched down to the unknown,
the loam, the moon-shy dark. You called, *Abstraction!*
as your fingers shaped into the word for five
but didn't pull your hand back from the black
of the abyss until the digits, still alive,
became just 5. You cried, *It's too abstract!*

when your arm snapped back: at the end of the limb
stood |5| which looked so vast but in fact was only
that which is not not five. At first you'd say
the skeleton had been the villain, blaming him,
but for the lure of the leap, the loss, though lonely.
In time, the hole transformed you all the way.

"I CAN SEE THROUGH WALLS"

—Arnold Schoenberg

I was forced into paradise, only
      Manzanita brush and citrus trees to numb me.
My music was murderous.

It killed the longing and closed the wound.

What holy voice roared, and who heard?
      If it is art, then it is not for all, and if it is
For all, then what future is this? Or what trick?

In exile, imagination waxes oracular, remembered

Silver willow trees hardly ballast for my destiny:
      To be *what no one wanted to be,*
What someone had to be, the emancipator

Of dissonance. I let it be me.

Even the present is shocking: the abuse and the music
      Badly played and labeled modern,
Music in search of love, music to transfigure night.

A prophet passing through a study of harmony,

I can see through walls. I fear 13.

I have to change your life with my dreams.

    *

But another time, we stopped for orange juice on Highway 1,
      My father and I, and we heard his "Verklärte Nacht" coming
Over a loudspeaker. I've never seen him so happy.

HOW THE LITTLE BEAR REFLECTED LIGHT

To Liliana Ursu

You said: "I've written no manifestos.
You can check my typewriter
if you'd like. I'll strike every key
for you, but keep in mind how
it degrades us both to verify."

You had a party when the word
loneliness was returned to you at last.
They had taken away your days
and your nights, but *loneliness* was back,
a large bright room with enough

space to kneel or lie flat
on the face and ask and wait.
By the way, I like waltz time, too.
Something dies after every three,
and then the one returns to you.

I came to Boston as a pilgrim,
not a Puritan, but still, I tried to find
a holy path. I circled the black box
of poetry, where the last words are
recorded. That indestructible box

in any sky. I came here for just
three things. I was ready to kneel
and pray for them. The idiom
of supplication opened like a cave.
I found fear only at the mouth of it.

*

I'd sought the wrong kind of angel.
I thought he'd be completely drenched
in beauty, but instead he was profane.
He reeked of yeast and brackish water.
His halo looked like lines drawn out

from the head, indicating pain.
When I found him we went deep
into the room of loneliness together.
The things we said were never written
down. I changed. You said: "go

to the place where your heart first beat."
I did. I took my pulse. I breathed.
And there I found the number three. Long
ago, I was born in a layer cake that stood
in the rain just above the beach.

A plane fell from the sky that day.
My father, brown eyes lashed above
his epaulets, piloted the plane. Through
the whole fiery crash, everyone was safe.
So first this: build a bridge to some

abyss, so I can stand to look at it:
statues on both sides, the fair dead
to the left and saints off to the right.
That second thing I found tonight:
your *lightwall* that I sought and sought

to be. St. Francis breathed inside your
poetry. I am named for a flower, too,
to live, die, and then be nothing here at all.
Why worry? I'm green even now, near
you, wearing my best disguise of blue.

*

Once with the filthy angel, I learned
a game of chance: I would jut my hand
out, flat like paper, shouting "poetry!"
and he would make a claw, and whisper
"ball of light," and grab the paper.

Or he'd extend a fist, and tell me,
"daily bread!" and I'd rest my paper
on the bread, to earn it. We went on
like this until the touching
of our hands became a fire.

But I chose "ball of light," and then
he went with "daily bread," and so
the game became inert. We sat down
to eat the bread, which, in the end, had
a baby in it, like a king cake. I named her

Liliana, after you. I put her in my pocket.
Then the bats flew in. I couldn't even
tell if they were real, but we fought them
with our poetry, our open hands waving
in the air. The angel left, but first

he brought his claw up to his chest,
to replace the ball of light. And me,
I rolled my poetry into a little
loaf of bread. In that bright room,
I held a child. That was the end.

I TYPED YOUR POEM WITH
MY OWN HANDS TODAY

The poem had a bird in it.
I didn't write it longhand, or in cursive.
It made me think of you
in Nebraska. You paused, and I felt it.
I had two windows open,
side by side as I typed.
It was the all-clean sensual experience you'd expect
from a futuristic movie starring Tom Cruise.
All the body parts, like *scar*, were clearly labeled.
I backspaced each time I made a mistake.
The poem came out ok.
In fact, it was moving. There were lines so ripe
I could have licked them.
It was an overtly political poem.
When you mentioned the bird the second time,
it was to save the bird.
But I could not reach out.
With my two hands on your hands, the poem
just streamed from my mouth.
The bird was suffering, covered in dirt.
More than hurt, the bird showed how soft
the real world sometimes is.
Not what I'd expected.
How awfully soft.

THE ANGEL IS AN AMALGAM

For Ladrea Icaza

In winter he wore a winter beard

He was sky high in the spring
His head grew light he let down the most

Delicate line he said get in the car
& on the ride a thick red book fell

From his *mouth like a lullaby*
He told how you crossed that chalky line

I didn't sleep I cried I curled
To the window on the passenger side

& just like that I remembered back
I asked him changer or destroyer?

He just narrowed his eyes and said
Forever in a wave like the pushy sound

A seashell makes then he slowed
His hand down the backs of my legs

And you know me I could not
Believe him but I was made smaller

For a time by desire   I was sorry
Lad I'm sorry because all this time

I never said your name
It thundered and when the angel said

Defenestration he pushed a flat
Hand to the side & I fell down fast

SMALL MACHINES WITH
SAPPHIC FRAGMENT

I baffled over and over you. Soft bellows in my chest
made whispers. Meanwhile, machines:
the laser strobed a dizzy disc, the silence of digital
kept time,
          fine filaments burned constantly in
a glass vacuum at the bedside. Eiderdown,
nightgown, *as long as you like* was the sound.

A SERIES OF HOLES
CONNECTED BY STRING

"When we obliterate nature and our bodies with polka dots,
we become part of the unity of our environments."
—Yayoi Kusama

A net, according to Samuel Johnson:
a series of holes connected by string,

the net of Indra faceted with jewels,
glittering web infinitely reflecting itself
and everything else, history told

by the victors, the story itself
a spoil. Yet the past is not a place.
You can't go home again, my Dad
so often said. He seemed to know

home as a time; he had been there
in mine. I've never yet let go of him
or you because you both were there:
your childhood, mine, epic light-drenched
vacation. The underwater world bright,

coral reefs infinite, and like everything else,
I often made it hard, but the water
reminded me I was no one. Born in the year
of the dog underneath a Sagittarius star,
I'm still a loyal wanderer, but oblivion gets in.
Once I love, it means ruin, but here I scatter

back into the present, bright fatherless regression
of offset mirrors, funny valentines, photographable
gemlike farewell lanterns cast onto the internet,
obliterated into pixels, disseminated
in liquid crystal before our bodies spoil.
I barely remember the islands,
the holes, a world now come to fire and ice.

II

In place of a hermeneutics we need an erotics of art.

—Susan Sontag, "Against Interpretation"

TREACHERY

It was not a pipe.
Nor a bowler hat.
We hadn't seen Tahiti,
Arles, or Guernica, nor the naked
Revelers of Spring all holding hands.
The camera changed that.

Later, when the big, soft blonde had died,
The coroner determined *not a suicide:*
The yellow jackets of the Nembutal
Were partially intact, in her stomach
And her throat, and underneath her arm
He found suspicious needle holes.
Suicide or hit, she passed
Completely into image after this.

SPECTRES

after Eva Hesse

Single Figure.

Working quickly,

A chest wound indicates distress beneath a huge orange hat.

Dyad.

Sisters, before. Chromatically twinned,

One is leaving; one stays.

A bride implied, roses at the center of a ballooning gown.

On the left, a masked shape turns away, leading with the center arm,

And the other has long ears, like a faun, and not of the present.

Triad.

Sisters and mother, afterward. Bodies underdeveloped.

One is slim and grey, in the background but impossible to paint out.

Rectangles indicate genitalia, or rectangles contain symbols indicating sex.

These don't describe something new, just something not yet known or touched.

The eye distortion indicates the weep and dominates.

The feet of another are oddly positioned, walking backward.

Single Figure.

Making, I learn to suffer better: yellow eyes, still life.

Do you know how to feel self-doubt without lashing out?

It's bottomless, no mouth.

"I WILL SEE THE FUTURE"

—Takashi Murakami

I.

Grotesquerie is not the right word.
Rather, bright colors!

I keep thinking: Peter, Peter,
don't codify us out of the experience.

Festivalists and fetishists, the
pathological, we are all lucky here:

still alive beneath an overcast sky.

The flat, factory finish on our desire,
the fantasies of fertilizing outer space

—method, commerce, millions: no
matter—this wall of eyes, it's the

purity you sought and could not find.

What an embarrassment of milks
will do, if you'd let your mouth relax.

2.

I'm lucky, just like him.
But I will probably go on living.

"Truth will out," they say.
For years, I've been vigilant.

It could come from anyone,
even the self.

It's like Magritte, only a grey sky
full of moles in blue suits.

I have seen the future a few times,
and it's so surprising.

I think, bright colors!
I think, bright eyes!

That is where my love lies /
my love lies.

And it's not like a movie,
where there's just one bad guy.

If you wait long enough, most
people are going to make a mistake.

So you start on forgiveness.
And that takes forever.

Starting in the past, whether or not
you knew about it,

and casting out to the love
that lies in your future self.

Still, for a while afterward,
I was embarrassed.

I guess I get a lot of it
from my Dad,

but he cannot see the future:
mushroom clouds and

mushroom suits, new kinds of music,
the way the angels live among us

in their ragged clothes, how the light
will reveal who we are.

THE MONOCLE IS A CIRCLE
THE EYE IS A CIRCLE

The monocle that walked with you
Rolled off the curb
Lay still in the wet leaves

Poems fell from the trees that year
Sugar crystals in their veins
Reminiscent of summer

Those leaves were a thousand fingers
In summer pointing this way and that
Until the road your companion got lost

Among a thousand arrows labeled *this way*
I remember you used thumb and flower
No, finger, to screw that lens

To your right eye
The late blooming flower of focus became you
Leaves drifted, until

LET US TRY FOR ONCE NOT TO BE RIGHT

I laughed and clapped
As my dog shat
On the neighbors' daffodils
I thought, when spring pushes, push back

It was March I was still here
Stitching up a small tear
In my heart   It was hard
Like sewing a button on a shirt

While you wear it
Like ironing a shirt
While you're wearing it
Using only the steam

When spring pushes push
Steam push pause push the door
Of the bedroom shut and mend
Tzara you were right the pink

Pill is ubiquitous is meaningless
Is All   The pink pill is the tear
Pushed from God's eye as he yelled
Up, whorish daffodils!

Sun, turn snow to rain to steam!

THE PROBLEM WITH SAMY ROSENSTOCK

You wrote me a book called *Scared Straight*, then *Nothing*, and then my favorite, *Sexy Math*. It's not like I was in love with you from the beginning. Or maybe I was. But a lot of other people were too, and that put me off. Plus, I had feelings for Tristan Tzara. In a Venn diagram, they would almost completely overlap. I'm sorry.

But Tzara died years ago, outside of Paris, gradually researching the snows, the codes of years passed. His poetry, his monocle, and his real name remain.

In *Sexy Math*, you explained why I can't get any closer to you. Each time I get halfway there, I think, "I'm halfway there!" I have a sip of water, fix my lipstick, and start out again. I get halfway there. This happens over and over. Usually, at some point I get hungry or take a nap. I've loved you this whole time, but I can't get there by half. And now I hear you're living in the extreme ultraviolet where only a moth or a baby could see you.

WHAT'S WATER?

This guy got lost in the snow. Then found.
Then came a sense of having lost the snow
or lost water or some infinite thing.

He watched the ME channel, day in and
day out. He couldn't help it. An old fish
swam by some little fish, asking,

How's the water? The skeletons in one
show taught parables about greed, envy,
and lust, to show how vices lead to loss.

A little rat got obsessed with
weightlifting and sex, for example.
She preened away, licking her tail and feet.

But the rat had already been lost, clearly,
or had already lost. From the beginning,
she'd looked thirsty. Her dark eyes peered out

as if toward some infinite thing, some body
of water from which to drink,
across which might be a horizon.

The guy remembered his time in Alaska
when, close to death, he had longed for God
with a purity that felt close to God, how

afterward the longing ebbed, and even
snow went back to being a hassle, often
dirty. The skeleton said, *Truth,* every time

the rat said, *Beauty.* In the wild, you melt snow
before you drink it. He had known that much,
to separate the air from water.

VALENTINE'S DAY AT THE SF MOMA, AGAIN

Most years, beyond LeWitt rainbows,
under Calder's mobile weights, past
Stieglitz's subjects, grey faces in grey worlds,
in a white gallery, red lifts from darkness.
A color field reverberates into an open eye.
It makes my heart pound, signaling nothing.

At fourteen, I arrived here knowing nothing,
arguably innocent, my hair curled up in bows.
Rothko took me through the eyes,
past Bullfinch, past an uprising of words, past
a poetry of silence, bent me to a dark
beginning, then I returned to a new world:

no chocolate, no candy, a red and longing world
I would later learn could pay me nothing
but this moment, a widening fissure, dark
delight of falling into the earth, or standing at the night ship's bow,
pulling ribbons from my hair, there to glide past
the fancy of content, the representative insult to the eye.

Once before, in the LA MOCA, we had a rendezvous: I
dissolved into four canvas walls, a world
of blue on blue.
Post-
metaphor, we were separated by nothing.
Someone bowed
on two strings, fretless, in the dark.

There is a red bridge over the dark
water—the crossing is called nostalgia, I
remember now—where the cellist took a bow

and translated, hotly from the underworld:
This trip, this song, will reduce you to nothing
if you open your eyes, if you look to the past.

Who knows how many Valentine's Days I've passed,
rushing past Klee and Diebenkorn to stand here until dark,
staring into my black and bleeding memory until there's nothing,
but *love, love, love . . . the soul of genius* on the eye?
Eventually, I shake my head and turn, rejoin the mobile world.
A man my age brushes past, turns and, patch-on-elbow,

asks, "What does it all mean?" Just go, get shot from that red bow,
past your interpretable world into the annihilating dark,
to return, arrow, into your own eye, white room meaning nothing.

III

And the place
was water

—Lorine Niedecker, "Paean to Place"

THE TRANSITIVE PROPERTIES OF SNOW

Tonight it snowed, copious, like
when I had chicken pox, all over
the night sky's skin and sickening.

Back home, you, inside my skin,
and a party with fake snow! There
I had a kind of freedom: *you are*

you, and I am me. It wasn't easy
to live like that, one body gazing out
at another, but I grew up in a warm place.

Then I got cold. I got a fever, and
the fever changed me. Now my
body slips into another, and I am full of love.

Birds of paradise stood in the window,
then the ocean and its moving boats.
My fidelities multiplied, not split,

but doubled and doubled again,
until thousands or more encircled us.
Magic, I said, looking up from the bed

as you stepped out. Now here I am,
way up North, lonely as a snowflake
in a sea of like shapes. There's a little

sand in my shoes and in my suitcase.
There's the light; there's the suitcase.
I finally understand a painting

I've seen of snow as paper cut-outs
strung on bare trees, to show the way
the world forgets itself so softly.

The light got under my skin. My hands
wave around the dark and net
through snowflakes. Strings break.

FEATHERS, QUIET, LIGHT

If only babies came from storks, I'd find a stork and have my baby. I'd march from the marsh, past the birdwatchers in their navy puffer jackets.

Sure, I know where babies come from. We'd *made love*, and by other names, for years. But it never worked right. No plus, no bellwether, no soft-emerging line.

Envision a totally white room. Now, quick, list three adjectives that describe that room. That's supposed to show how you feel about death. For me, it's more like living alone, which I mostly enjoy.

Walking in my shiny shoes, first one foot, then the other, all my worry counteracts my hope.

I MAKE THE LIVING WATER WET

You knew, seeking a home, it was beneath you
Pulsing like a Greek ideal,
But things don't appear
To move toward the good,
                              that part erroneous.

Quatrains run heavy,
The sea underneath you four days on and time
   much more precious now.
I solidify the sea to hold the boat.
I make the living water wet.

I feather and fur the fauna. Then I inlay the fret.
You seek and in seeking cannot find, but sing.
The home fantasy battles the birds
                              between an implied moon and those
                              godlike rays of sun.
Still sing, stop, swim, run.

PROTEAS

Here, find a barrel-chested, barrel-chasing
Proteas, ambivalent against various coastlines,

Jellyfish, and birds of paradise. Just kids
When we met, we leapt from the pier in the night;

He swam ahead, and when I lost sight of shore,
His friend brought me in from the tide.

At first, desire was not enough, but as we grew,
It became a world—myth, anima, and stand—

When we crossed paths. In Fiji, coral-cut
And grieving, *I don't know* became his new horizon

Line. Alone in the boat—I followed it home.
Water soaked my hair, my feet, and clothes.

I never glanced back, except in memory, where,
Nights, he returns the serves of a machine

Under mercury lights at the old high school,
Eyeing the waves, trying to stay in shape.

VITA ASTRALE

In my dream you entered naked, out of shape.
It was the mood of focused human sex.
After a while, you grew surly, sat back against
the head of the bed and made a comment
in some ugly way. I said no, it's not like that.
I love you, or, I loved you. I can't remember
which. And you began to cry, red-faced, serious.
I said don't cry; we're here right now. But
you, even in the dream, remembered, asked,
How long have you been married? I wanted
to tell the wonder of my daughter and ask
you not to visit me this way. Instead
I touched your chest and said, I married shortly
after we last met. You wept. I wept.

THE HALF-GOD APPEARS

You, agnostic,
standing in god-light at the edge of the wood,

sense the pulse,
say: *truth, tiny, partial, contingent.*

Have you been looking for your maker
but longing to live?

I met the half-god;
his mother was human she had tears in her eyes.

Or, he came from the back world;
he had tears in his eyes.

He suggested "hold on," a way to die.

*

Suggestion: astonishment.
Suggestion: fruitless waiting.

Encoded in the problem of the 20th century,
from which I emerged,

tiny dots formed the figure on horseback:
not form but the marrow of form.

The half-god is graceless,
but an arrow can't kill him.

The half-god points
to your false hope of fulfillment.

He emerged from the back world, eyes devoid of tears.

*

The horseback figure obscures the daytime
clouds and the pillar of fire.

He is seen by the unseen and overlooked by God.
The half-god reminds you

that you are still waiting,
empty belly and eyes intent on the leaves.

This half-god could be fought with flowers
and rejoicing, but who can?

This is what he took down
open-mouthed, lance drawn:

cool nights spent in the garden out behind the house,

*

the honeysuckle vines, the garden wall, the house.
Or was it the waiting that tore them down?

The pink pill was the promise,
the capsule broke open, the dots formed the figure:

he emerged from the shadow of the wood
in a lullaby

translated variously as: jealousy, the ground
falling away from the feet, anxiety.

Suggestion: abandon all hope.
Suggestion: "no one said you wouldn't be changed."

I WAS READING UP ON MY HELLENIC MATH

I was reading up on my Hellenic math: no zero yet, no transfinite set theory, no *sine* or *cosine*, just a Brotherhood that felt divine to its practitioners. You were back in California, riding on the waves, your father gone awhile, and me, you said, no consolation outside of the bed. I've never yet let go of zero, the multiplier best employed on incommensurate sums, either one on top a lovelier ratio, but when divided through becomes a number that can't compute, but instead goes on, in proof, diminished by each digit that it spews.

Eudoxus did not quite anticipate you, a curve that skims but will not touch the bottom line. And then the Romans came, and all was lost for quite some time.

IV

for you alone the unseen signal will come
to force your way among the light ways

—Tristan Tzara, "Palm Grove"
  (trans. Lee Harwood)

NEW NAMES

I.

Our gazes met and wove a filament aflame
In the warm vacuum of our acquaintance.

In the steam heat, central heat, and blue light
Of a flea-bitten house, dizzy, we fell down.

We tore the night, fought fear with fear.
I left the house, running around with the ghosts

In the unfamiliar South. We held fast, each
Of us lost in hope, grotesque, as we lost

The first one, little weight, until the faces
In the vapor dissipated and the house emptied

Out of time. When we found traces of life
We recognized, we broke the tender void

Between our hands and made it new, not
Like poetry, but more like plants or seasons

On the Earth, and it sounded us new names.

2. *I Have Gazed upon the Face of*_____

Gold grave goods and lion gates at Mycenae,
Masks but not quite Agamemnon's face,

The Ionian Sea, Argolic Gulf, old Nafplio,
Cape Tenaro, and you, in the courthouse,

Trembling, responding, "Ne!" to everything
The deputy mayor said: "Yes," we will teach

Our children to be good citizens, to read.
In the leather ledger we penned new names,

Then walked into the midday blaze,
Our marriage not the culmination of love,

But a call to love. My love, afraid, masked
And unmasked in your gaze, lonely hilltop

Ruins were the place we bravely sang
Strangers to each other, two and one,

The wind off the water filling us up with power.

3. *Birth*

There is no mist like this mist.
No smoking. No mistakes. No
unkind words. Just change.

Water breaks.
There is no crystal quite like this.
This is how we get our names.

Fluttering belly-bound babe.
I grew up so I could take
care. Take care of you.

Little bundle stuck for a while—
Peter's eyes—I found
a cave in my mind, and pushed.

Your mouth a brown rectangle
of sound, just after you came out.
Blue eye on mine, nursing, round.

4. *Giardino di Ninfa*

We found a dogwood tree in Italy,
Flowering among the nymphs.

Green water: we know spring
Is coming, while there's still time.

I've been oblique or buried,
Enduring the opulence of the villa,

Like a scrap of *spoglia*, half-
Inscribed, my message unalive.

For years, one question in the manic
Diagram of my own life: *who died?*

But I had it wrong. Swelling
With child while the ice melts,

I hear you say: *we die.* It's not
A question, and it's present tense.

Still, we're done waging shadow play
With death this year. We know spring

Is coming, while there's still time.
We've carried one another

To the center of our lives, where
We can't see our lives, but see a view,

Great stone pines and Roman roofs.
One line whispers into another line.

SPOGLIE

Sculptures are embedded in the wall, human
Forms reclined onto their sides
To properly incorporate them to the scene.
A cross etched into a stone
That was, according to my guidebook,
Once used in pagan rituals. It's practical
To reuse columns, blocks, and old reliefs.
Some apotropaic magic does the trick,
Wards away the evil eye, deflects
Bad luck from all the walls or entrance halls
Or sacred rooms. Victors choose
The semiology, reuse the rubble,
Reconsecrate the grounds.
My love for you is made
Out of my old love for you.

ROME, WITH CHILD

I have run toward the shrinking light
of the future, ignoring whirlwinds and waves.
I bore a child into this light,

an act of hubris, perhaps, or selfishness
followed by untold tenderness.
It slowed me down.

Then I moved from the new world
to the old, where the many pasts pile up
roadside, covered in green things growing.

At night I nurse my child while by iPhone
light I read about the stones, the salvaged
columns, and Augustus, Nero,

Constantine, and Hannibal, his elephants
approaching warlike from the north,
another particular end of a world.

Or secret churches inside houses back
when Christianity was a subversive force.
I wander churches, watching Mary

in each image hold her glowing child.
In some, she makes a gesture with her hand
to indicate she speaks, she teaches, she can

read and preach. My daughter points to baby
angels in the paintings and the friezes on the walls;
she points out Baby Jesus in each crèche,

and I realize, agnostic, this sanctification
of procreation, this story of the babe announced,
arrived, and glorified, is ours:

we're born, we grow, we bear some measure
of humiliation and betrayal, and we die.
Our mothers watch some portion of these lives,

and in our minds they glow.
We are haloed.
I am surprised

when I find I'm in the family way again.
Here, among stone pines and olive trees
from long ago, I start again. My body swells

and breaks, my mind a dry rubble waiting
for a rain of sleep. I had been moving forward,
with my girl, her growing up, and now

we slide into a new kind of time. Walking
to the doctor on the cobblestones between
two ancient walls, I narrow my scope

to try to see one smile, to hear one funny word
from the girl, to try to believe in a continuity
of things, not only forward motion.

The cats, of course, cover all these ruins,
each colony distinct, camped for generations
in one monument or field, come rain or shine.

O, TO LIVE IN THE NECROPOLIS

A graffiti-laden crypt to call my own, wandering
The lanes of those passed into the living document,

And when I joke with you like this, I'm totally sincere
But totally deluded, because I want to live.

The arrogance of the healthy, to mutter "kill me now"
To the bank teller moving slowly at her tasks,

But the healthy must enjoy life by forgetting they'll
Surely lose it, though that's in the margins all the while.

In truth, I live inside the city of the dead some of the time.
The place you love, can you be there and not be there, too?

Bright colors, what would be called exaggerated hues,
Were they not true, are used to make the living proof.

I'm not a mother in this place, or a wife to you, but
I want to talk about our work with you. Leaving home,

I wonder why. Then hurry to get back by dinner time.
But, still, I want to move around some leaves,

To cultivate or compost some luscious patch of dirt
Beside this mausoleum that lies in wait for me.

I search myself for love: what once was green
Is now just filled with ache. I ask, I order,

And I exclaim, studying the language, reading,
And then listening again. On one hand, truth.

And on the other, wild milk fertilizing planets.
Between these, a mossy chasm called necropolis.

A basilica on a basilica on a church above a graveyard
Which covers a necropolis built upon a circus where ancient

Races and atrocities occurred: and in that layer-cake
An unknown woman's bones still rest in Peter's crypt.

Do you invent by necessity or for the thrill of it? Do
You prefer the titillation of the silk or the sweat-soaked

Aftermath? Does your performance satisfy your muse,
And could you really know? The arrogance of the vision,

To offer consolation to each wretch, even those who
Break and never, ever break, showing their protean

Tormentors what it takes to stay in shape—I wanted
To believe, inside the basilica. But I was found out.

Believe my questions, my orders, and my shouts. Believe
My doubt. I have no manifesto, nor the faith I'd need.

I searched for something green, but found only a map
Of the burial place. Making maps of music, of books,

Of time, I meditate to get to know my mind.
I'd like to put things back in place. What escapes

The streets of that still and buried city? The high and alive.
What marginalia saved you when you were on the brink

And coughing? Could you recreate your epiphany
So it can be laid, carefully, in that burial place beneath

The world's eye where we are stupefied or crucified
Or petrified at last, eternal. Quiet? Quiet. What a lovely

Word, if you can hear it rising up, over the din
Of everything but your heartbeat. I'm here,

Saying, take me to the city of the dead where
I will live as one with trees and water. I mean

Take me past the trees and water and into milky
Space with poets humming silently along. I am yet

Inside this life: green bloom, red walls, white bones,
The aperture.

FABLE FOR A GENOME

After David Ferry

In the sculpture, Aeneas wore a helmet, held
his son's hand, and carried his thin father,
weathered and wild-eyed, but alive. My father

was bearded and wild-eyed before he died.
My son was ten days old and sleeping all the time,
and though I do not pray I knew if only one

could live, it should be him, little belly little
brain, hand curled tight around my finger
as I nursed him down to sleep then drove

the unlit road back to the ICU to find my dad
now clutching at the family gods and spitting: back!
at an approaching nurse, and then to me, quietly:

who can I trust? as I harangued the doctors
for more drugs. I could not carry him away,
and like Aeneas, I made mistakes. He died. *A whole*

library burned down. The myth of my autonomy
began to fade from my own system of belief.
Instead, a chemical intelligence was using me—

mother, daughter, vehicle—to change and recombine,
each body cast aside in time. I washed my hands
in running water. I changed clothes in the garage

beside the washer. I watched everybody sleep.
Some carried their fathers on their backs, some
fled with children from wasted cities and armed attacks.
What can't be carried can be scattered on the water.

NOTES

The phrase *sprinting up the hill* in "If Anything Is Everlasting It Can Only Be One Thing" comes from Elizabeth Kolbert's *The Sixth Extinction.*

The phrase *wholeness, radiance, harmony* in "Provincial Time" is from James Joyce via James Longenbach's *The Art of the Poetic Line.*

"Aristotle Is a Skeleton" takes its title from Wallace Stevens' "Adagia."

The title "I Can See through Walls" is a quotation, possibly apocryphal, from Arnold Schoenberg. Phrases in this poem are borrowed from Alex Ross's *The Rest is Noise,* and the final, italicized section is a quotation from Schoenberg's son.

A few short phrases in "The Angel Is an Amalgam" are taken from Frank Stanford's *The Battlefield Where the Moon Says I Love You.*

Phrases in "Spectres" are borrowed from Eva Hesse's letters and notebooks.

"I Will See the Future" riffs off Peter Schjeldahl's *New Yorker* review of a 2007 Takashi Murakami retrospective.

"Let Us Try for Once Not to Be Right" is a quote from Tristan Tzara's "Dada Manifesto," as translated by Robert Motherwell.

"Valentine's Day at the SF MOMA, Again" borrows some language from Susan Sontag's essay "Against Interpretation."

"I Make the Living Water Wet" takes its title from *The Upanishads,* as quoted in David Lynch's *Catching the Big Fish.*

Language in "The Half-God Appears" is borrowed from Theodore Adorno and Friedrich Nietzsche as quoted in Adorno's *Metaphysics Concepts and Problems.*

The phrase "a whole library burned down" in "Fable for a Genome" refers to Swedish artist Susanna Hesselberg's art installation "When My Father Died It Was Like a Whole Library Had Burned Down," which draws its title from a Laurie Anderson song, "World Without End."

ACKNOWLEDGMENTS

Thanks, for insight and encouragement, to Cynthia Arrieu-King, Adam Eaglin, Martin Eisner, Caroline Sterne Falzone, Angela Gregg, Dave Madden, Kristin Naca, Neal Nuttbrock, Adam Peterson, Vanesha Pravin, Mathias Svalina, and Saskia Ziolkowski. I'm grateful to my teachers Maggie Dietz, Louise Glück, Ted Kooser, Hilda Raz, and Robert Pinsky. Special thanks to Mathias and Robert for your words here. Grazie to the American Academy in Rome for allowing me time to work as a visiting artist, and to friends there with whom, as a "fellow traveler," I was lucky to explore. I'm grateful to my students and colleagues at George Mason, especially Jennifer Atkinson, Suzanne Carbonneau, Sally Keith, and Eric Pankey. To Mary Green, thank you for everything.

Thanks to Mary Biddinger, Amy Freels, and everyone at University of Akron Press, and to Kevin Francis Gray, for permission to use this image of his sculpture for the cover. I'm grateful to Daniel Lin at Love Among the Ruins, who published some of these poems in the chapbook *No Omen*, and to the editors of the following journals, who first published many of these poems: *AGNI online*, *Barrelhouse*, *Bennington Review*, *Blackbox Manifold*, *Boog City*, *Boxcar Poetry Review*, *Ekleksographia*, *Everyday Genius*, *Lungfull!*, *New Yorker*, *RealPoetik*, and *Sixth Finch*.

This collection is dedicated to Peter Streckfus, in love and deep gratitude; you carried me through.

Heather Green is the author of two chapbooks, *No Omen* and *The Match Array*, and the translator of two collections of Tristan Tzara's poetry: *Noontimes Won* (Octopus Books, 2018) and *Guide to the Heart Rail* (Goodmorning Menagerie, 2017). Her poems have appeared in *Bennington Review*, *Denver Quarterly*, the *New Yorker*, and elsewhere, and her translations of Tzara's work have appeared in *Asymptote*, *Poetry International*, and several anthologies. She teaches in the School of Art at George Mason University.

Printed in the United States
By Bookmasters